HISTORY MAKERS

TUDORS
and
STUARTS

PEGGY BURNS

ILLUSTRATED BY

JESSICA CURTIS

Wayland

HISTORY MAKERS

History Makers of the Middle Ages
History Makers of the Second World War
Tudors and Stuarts
Victorians

Notes for teachers

History Makers uses a wide range of exciting contemporary sources – quotations, letters, paintings and artefacts – to build up detailed and informative portraits of people who made important contributions both to their own time and to the way we live now.

This book:

- features important figures from all areas of Tudor and Stuart life – science and technology, the arts, exploration, war, education and health;

- presents contemporary reactions to changes and innovations;

- focuses on Tudor and Stuart society and the changes and developments that occurred within it;

- emphasizes the importance of Tudor and Stuart achievements for modern life.

First published in 1994 by Wayland
(Publishers) Ltd
61 Western Road, Hove, East Sussex
BN3 1JD, England

© Copyright 1994 Wayland (Publishers) Ltd

Series editor: Katie Roden
Series designer: Tracy Gross
Book designer: Joyce Chester

British Library Cataloguing in Publication Data

Burns, Peggy
Tudors and Stuarts. – (History Makers Series)
I. Title II. Curtis, Jessica III. Series
941.05

ISBN 0-7502-1266-7

Typeset by Dorchester Typesetting Group Ltd
Printed and bound in Italy by Rotolito

Picture acknowledgements:

British Library 12; British Museum 11, 41; Mary Evans Picture Library 23 (top), 24 (top), 30 (both), 43; Eye Ubiquitous 38; Chris Fairclough 35 (bottom); Fotomas 6, 9, 14, 16 (bottom); Magdalene College, Cambridge 28; Mansell Collection 16 (top), 33; Museum of London 29, 31, 34 (bottom); National Portrait Gallery 10, 22; Peter Newark's Historical Pictures 38; Photostage (Donald Cooper) 17 (bottom); Public Records Office 17 (top); Wayland Picture Library 9, 13, 18, 19, 20 (both), 21, 23 (bottom), 24 (top), 25, 26, 27, 32, 35 (top), 36, 37 (both); Weaversmith 15; Woodmansterne Ltd 34 (top).

C o n t e n t s

Words in **bold** in the text can be found in the
Glossary on page 44.

Anne Boleyn

1507 – 1536

'I have been more than one year now struck by the dart of love…'

Anne Boleyn's heart must have beaten faster as she read her love letter, because the man writing to her was Henry VIII, the king of England. The king was in love with her, and wanted to marry her. The trouble was, he was already married.

Henry and his wife, Queen Catherine, only had a daughter, Mary. More than anything else, Henry wanted a son who could be king after his own death. Now, a clever, well-educated young woman, Anne Boleyn, who had come to the king's court from France, had captivated Henry.

Henry forced his bishops to accept him as head of the Church in England instead of the Pope in Rome. This picture shows him crushing the Pope – the artist wanted to show how strong Henry's will was.

He showered gifts on her: jewellery, land and money. He wanted to marry Anne desperately – but Queen Catherine was in the way. The only answer was **divorce**.

Most people in England at that time, including King Henry, were **Catholics**. Henry asked the Pope in Rome, who was head of the Church, for a divorce. When the Pope refused, Henry decided to go ahead and divorce Catherine anyway. He broke away from the Catholic church and said that in future, the king or queen would be head of the Church of England, a tradition which is still true today.

Anne became pregnant, and Henry married her secretly even before he was legally divorced from Catherine. So Anne became queen of England.

Her **coronation** in the Church of Westminster was magnificent. Archbishop Cranmer, who crowned her as queen, wrote:

'We received the Queen apparelled (dressed) in a robe of purple velvet and all the ladies and gentlewomen in robes and gowns of scarlet.'

Henry was sure she would give him the son he so badly wanted. The baby, when it was born, was healthy and strong – but it was a girl, Elizabeth. Henry was angry and disappointed. The next child, Anne promised him, would be a boy. But two years passed, and there were no more babies. Anne grew fearful. The king's patience – like his love – was wearing thin.

At last, Anne became pregnant again. This child must be a boy. But when Anne had a **miscarriage** and the son they longed for never had a chance of life, she knew that all was lost.

Henry decided to rid himself of Anne so that he could marry someone else. He said that Anne was a witch, and accused her of **adultery**. She was arrested and imprisoned in the Tower of London.

Even before the trial, Henry had made up his mind to get rid of her. She was condemned to die on the **scaffold**.

On the morning of her execution, she wrote a last letter to Henry:

'To speak a truth, never a prince had a wife more loyal in all duty and in all affection than you have ever found, in Anne Boleyn.'

DATE CHART

1509
Henry VIII comes to the throne.

1522
Anne Boleyn comes to the court and is banished to Hever Castle by Cardinal Wolsey.

1526
Anne returns to the court.

1527
Henry asks for a divorce.

1532
Anne becomes pregnant.

1533
25 January: Henry secretly marries Anne.
May: divorce from Catherine is granted.

1533
7 September: Elizabeth is born.

1535
Anne becomes pregnant again.

1536
January: Anne miscarries her child.

1536
19 May: Anne is beheaded.

OTHER WIVES OF HENRY VIII

Catherine of Aragon
Jane Seymour
Anne of Cleves
Catherine Howard
Catherine Parr

Lady Jane Grey
1537 – 1554

'I think myself in hell…!'

Roger Ascham, who was a tutor to the royal family and was visiting the young Lady Jane Grey, listened sadly as the teenager poured out her dread of her strict parents.

Lady Jane's only hours of real happiness were when she was learning. She was especially good at Latin and Greek. She was very clever, and her teacher was a kind, gentle man. She told Ascham unhappily:

'When I am called from him, I fall on weeping, because whatsoever I do else but learning is full of grief, trouble, fear, and whole misliking unto me.'

When Jane was fifteen her parents forced her to marry Guildford Dudley, a young man she hated. But they and Guildford's parents had plans for the young couple that Jane knew nothing about.

Jane was a cousin of the sick young king, Edward VI, the son of Henry VIII and his third wife, Jane Seymour. Now the boy king was dying. Who would reign after his death? Edward had two half-sisters: Princess **Mary Tudor**, the eldest (who was Henry's daughter by his first queen, Catherine) and Elizabeth (Anne Boleyn's daughter).

Princess Mary should have been queen after Edward, but many did not want her, because she was a Catholic. Edward was a **Protestant**. And Lady Jane Grey, his cousin, was also a Protestant. The dying young king was persuaded to sign a will naming Jane as queen after his death.

A short time later, Edward died, and Jane was declared queen.

Jane was horrified. She did not want the throne. She knew that Mary should now be queen. But in the end she let herself be persuaded. Perhaps, Jane told herself, this was God's will for her life?

But Mary, also, knew that *she* should be queen . . . and so did many others. People rushed to support Mary and turned against the new queen Jane. Within days, the plot to put Jane on the throne had failed, and her own father had her arrested. Jane, together with her husband, was condemned to death.

Carrying a prayer book, the sixteen-year-old girl walked calmly out to the scaffold, where the executioner, with his axe, waited by the block.

A bystander later described the scene:

'The (executioner) kneeled down, and asked her forgiveness, whom she forgave most willingly. Then he willed her to stand upon the straw: which doing, she saw the block. Then she said, "I pray you dispatch me quickly".'

One of her ladies handed Jane a scarf, which she tied around her eyes. There was a moment of panic as she felt for the block with her hands, and couldn't find it. 'What shall I do?' she cried. 'Where is it?'

'One of the standers-by guiding her thereunto, she laid her head down upon the block, and stretched forth her body and said: "Lord, into thy hands I commend my spirit".'

Young, clever and beautiful, Jane Grey, queen for only nine days, died because of greedy people's desire for power and wealth.

DATE CHART

1537
Jane Grey is born.

1553
25 May: Jane is forced to marry Lord Guildford Dudley.

1553
June: Edward VI is persuaded to sign a will leaving the crown to Jane.

1553
6 July: King Edward dies.

1553
10 July: Jane is proclaimed queen. Mary flees to East Anglia.

1553
19 July: Mary is recognized as queen. Jane is put under arrest.

1554
12 February: Jane is beheaded.

OTHERS TO STUDY

King Edward VI
Mary Tudor

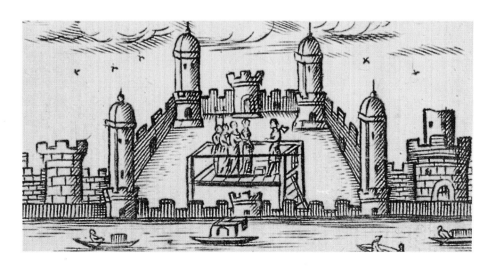

Lady Jane Grey went to her death with great courage.

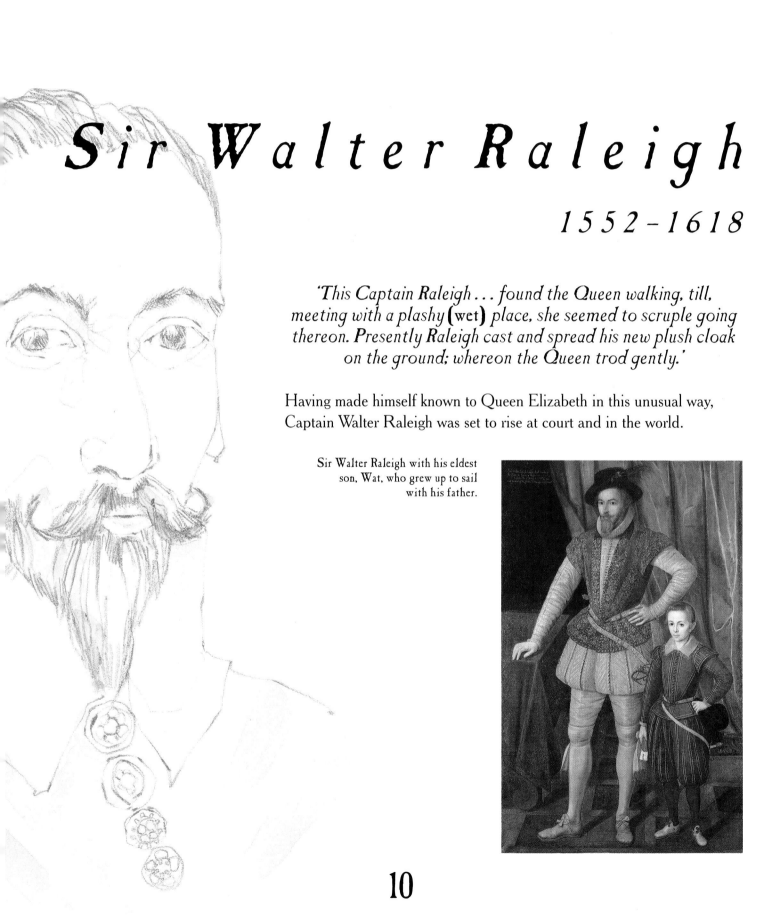

Sir Walter Raleigh

1552 – 1618

'This Captain Raleigh ... found the Queen walking, till, meeting with a plashy (wet) place, she seemed to scruple going thereon. Presently Raleigh cast and spread his new plush cloak on the ground; whereon the Queen trod gently.'

Having made himself known to Queen Elizabeth in this unusual way, Captain Walter Raleigh was set to rise at court and in the world.

Sir Walter Raleigh with his eldest son, Wat, who grew up to sail with his father.

Raleigh was a brilliant soldier, daring and full of courage. He was also bold and romantic, and wrote poetry. He soon became one of the queen's favourites – though his arrogant manner made a lot of people at court dislike him. He became rich and powerful.

Though he was talented in many ways, Raleigh's great interest was exploration. He wanted to look for lands across the sea and claim them for England.

A picture of two native Americans in Virginia, by John White, a sixteenth-century explorer.

He spent much of his new wealth sending ships to North America, trying to get English people to go and live there in a place he called Virginia. The voyage was not a success, though. All Raleigh had to show for it were potatoes and tobacco – new plants found in Virginia that had never been seen before in England.

Raleigh's great dream was to find gold. He had heard of a golden city in the South American region of Guiana called El Dorado. He had heard that the emperor there was so rich that he used gold-dust to powder his body.

Raleigh fitted out more ships and sailed south, determined to find El Dorado, and the mines where the gold and silver were believed to come from.

11

DATE CHART

1552
Raleigh is born.

1582
Comes to Queen Elizabeth I's court.

1584
6 January: knighted by Elizabeth.
Elizabeth grants him a charter to send ships to found a British colony in North America. He calls it Virginia.

1588
Takes part in the fight against the Spanish Armada.

In Guiana, the English often treated the native South Americans as
slaves, even though Raleigh himself tried to respect them.

The native South Americans were friendly towards Raleigh and his
men. Raleigh respected them and did them no harm, even though most
English people believed that they were uncivilized and ignorant.

In small boats, the party threaded their way up the Orinoco River
towards the fabled city. But, burnt by the hot sun and with his supplies
running short, Raleigh was forced to turn back.

He later wrote, in a book about his voyage:

*'I never saw a more beautiful country, nor more lively prospects
… the air fresh with a gentle easterly wind, and every stone that
we stooped to take up promised either gold or silver.'*

Raleigh's life changed when the new king, James I (James VI of
Scotland), came to the English throne. From the beginning he and
Raleigh disliked each other. Raleigh spoke against the king and ended up
in the Tower of London under sentence of death for **treason**.

But Raleigh did not die – yet. On the very morning of the
execution, King James stopped it from going ahead. The king needed
money desperately, and he had heard Raleigh's stories of 'rich and
beautiful cities . . . temples adorned with golden images . . . filled with
treasure'.

Though he had never seen the city of El Dorado for himself,
Raleigh still believed that it was to be found. He persuaded the king to
allow him to make one more voyage to search for gold.

Raleigh set sail, but at sixty-four he had lost the energy of his youth. He was weakened by his years in prison, and partly paralysed from a sudden illness.

On arriving in Guiana, he sent a large force of men ashore, but they were attacked by Spanish **colonists** (England and Spain were old enemies). Many men – including Sir Walter's son, Wat – were killed. Those who escaped sailed up the Orinoco but found no city, and no gold. They returned to their ships with only half their men still alive. Raleigh ordered them to go on with the search, but they refused.

Mourning the loss of his son and sick with disappointment at his failure, Sir Walter Raleigh sailed home to England, to meet his own death on the scaffold for treason.

Having failed in his quest for El Dorado, Raleigh prepares to die on the scaffold.

1595
Sails to Guiana.

1603
Elizabeth dies.

1603
Imprisoned by James I.

1603
Execution sentence is delayed.

1617
Sets sail on his final voyage.

1618
Raleigh is executed.

13

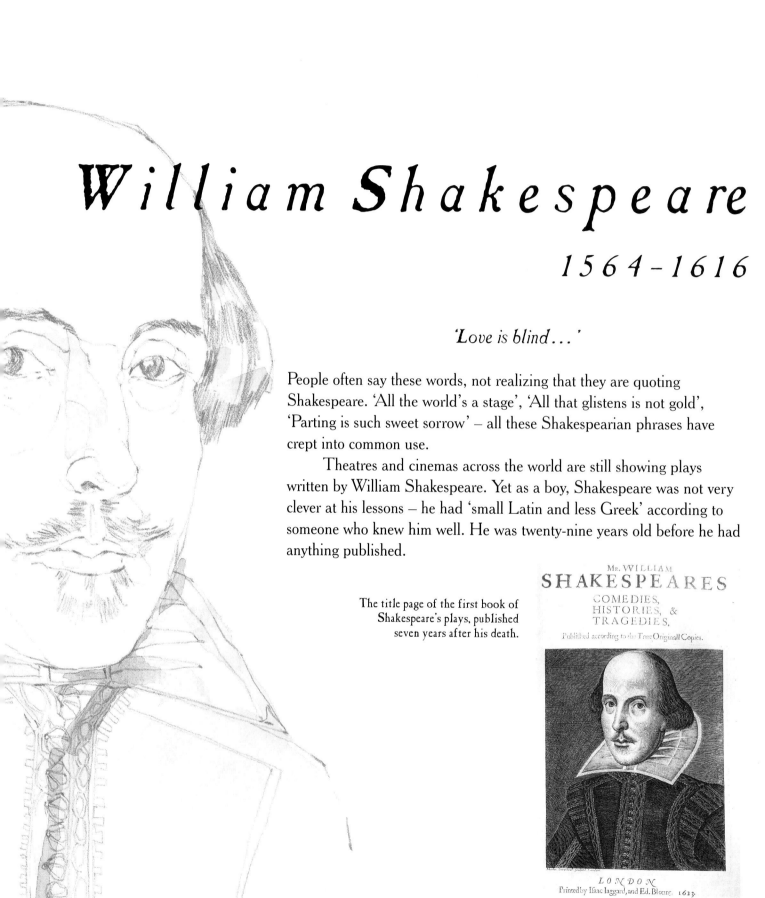

William Shakespeare

1564-1616

'Love is blind...'

People often say these words, not realizing that they are quoting Shakespeare. 'All the world's a stage', 'All that glistens is not gold', 'Parting is such sweet sorrow' – all these Shakespearian phrases have crept into common use.

Theatres and cinemas across the world are still showing plays written by William Shakespeare. Yet as a boy, Shakespeare was not very clever at his lessons – he had 'small Latin and less Greek' according to someone who knew him well. He was twenty-nine years old before he had anything published.

The title page of the first book of Shakespeare's plays, published seven years after his death.

MR. WILLIAM
SHAKESPEARES
COMEDIES,
HISTORIES, &
TRAGEDIES.

Published according to the True Originall Copies.

LONDON
Printed by Isaac Iaggard, and Ed. Blount. 1623.

He could not have guessed at that time that he would one day be the most famous playwright ever known, or that phrases he had written would become part of everyday speech.

How many times have you been told, 'You're eating me out of house and home'? Adults say it now, but Shakespeare said it first!

William Shakespeare grew up in Stratford-upon-Avon, England, where his father was the mayor. At the age of eighteen he married Anne Hathaway, who was eight years older than himself. In his early twenties he left Stratford for London, where he met poets and actors.

Plays were performed with little or no scenery, and all the female characters were acted by boys.

Shakespeare was well liked by most people who knew him. Ben Jonson, another playwright, wrote that he was 'honest, and of an open and free nature.' Someone else described him as 'handsome . . . well-shaped,' and said that he had 'a very ready and pleasant, smooth wit'.

Before long, William Shakespeare was famous in London. He became an actor with a company of players, later sharing the profits. He became wealthy, bought a large house in Stratford, and was part-owner of a new playhouse, The Globe, in London.

Fifteen years later, The Globe had a sad ending. During the first performance of *Henry VIII* some of the scenery caught fire and within a couple of hours the whole theatre had burnt to the ground.

Nobody died in the blaze – and though the fire was a terrible blow to Shakespeare and the other owners, it had moments of humour. One of the audience wrote later:

'Nothing did perish but wood and straw, and a few forsaken cloaks; only one man had his breeches set on fire, that would perhaps have broiled him, if he had not by the benefit of a provident wit put it out with a bottle of ale.'

OTHERS TO STUDY

Ben Jonson
– a playwright and poet.
Christopher Marlowe
– a playwright and poet.
David Garrick
–a famous actor.
John Donne
– a poet and preacher.
Sir Francis Bacon
– a writer.

The Globe

Shakespeare lived to see The Globe Theatre rebuilt.

Shakespeare wrote an enormous number of plays and verses on many different subjects. Some of his plays were historical, some were tragic, others were very funny. His plays were enjoyed by Queen Elizabeth I, and, after her death, by King James I.

In his late forties, William Shakespeare decided to leave London to live the life of a retired gentleman in Stratford.

A drawing of Shakespeare's house in Stratford.

16

In his last play, *The Tempest*, he wrote about death:

'We are such stuff
As dreams are made on, and our little life
Is rounded with a sleep.'

Shakespeare's will; look at his shaky signature. Even three hundred years after his death, his plays are still performed all over the world. Below is a production of *A Comedy Of Errors*.

Shakespeare never recovered from the shock of the blaze at The Globe. Though he lived to see it rebuilt, he died – many believe of a fever – on what is thought to have been his fifty-second birthday.

Shakespeare's plays are still read for pleasure, studied for examinations, acted on stages, produced in films and even made into cartoons. And though he lived so long ago, Shakespeare is still remembered today as a great genius. His marvellous works were his gift to the whole world.

G u y   F a w k e s

1 5 7 0 – 1 6 0 6

'Remember, remember, the fifth of November,
Gunpowder treason and plot.
I see no reason why gunpowder treason
Should ever be forgot.'

So goes the old rhyme which even today is chanted every year on
5 November, when models of Guy Fawkes are burnt at bonfire parties all
around Britain.

The eye of God watches as
Guy Fawkes sneaks towards
the Houses of Parliament.

Gun Powder Treafon.

18

Fawkes and his fellow plotters.

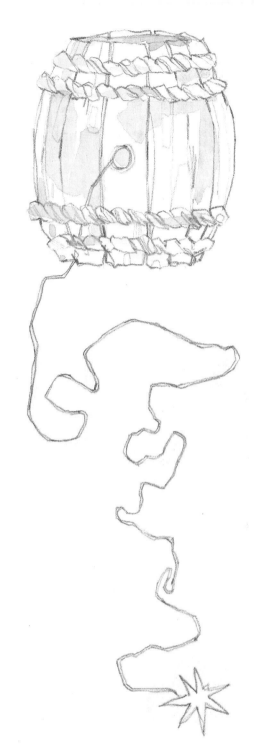

Bonfire Night celebrates the discovery of a plot to blow up the **House of Lords** on 5 November, 1605. The plotters hoped to kill King James I and his eldest son, Prince Henry. Fireworks are let off to remind people of the gunpowder Guy Fawkes planned to use.

The plot that went badly wrong – fortunately for the king and his **Parliament** – had been carefully planned out in every detail for many months.

James I was a Protestant king. Britain had been Protestant since the end of 'Bloody' Mary Tudor's reign, but there were still many Catholics in Britain. A man called Robert Catesby and a few others believed that Britain should be Catholic once more. They thought that if they blew up the House of Lords there would be nobody left to rule the country.

They planned to kidnap the king's younger son, five-year-old Prince Charles, rule the country themselves in his name, and return Britain to the Catholic faith.

Some members of the House of Lords, however, were Catholics themselves . . . and it was because of them that Catesby's gang made their fatal mistake. The plotters didn't want their Catholic friends and relatives to die. So some of them were warned to avoid the House of Lords on 5 November.

One morning at the end of October, Lord Monteagle, a Catholic nobleman, received a mysterious unsigned letter:

*'Retire yourself into the country, where you may expect the event in safety, for though there be no appearance of any stir, yet I say they shall receive a terrible blow this **Parliament**, and yet they shall not see who hurts them.'*

19

my lord out of the loue i beare to some of youer frendz i haue acaer of youer preseruacion Therfor I would aduyse yowe as yowe tender youer lyf to deuyse some effcuse to shift of youer attendance at this parleament for god and man hathe concurred to punishe the wickednes of this tyme and thinke not slightlye of this aduertisment but retere youre self into youre contri wheare yowe maye expect the euent in safti for thowyge theare be no apparance of anni stir yet i saye they shall receyue a terrible blowe this parleament and yet they shall not seie who hurts them this councel is not to be contemned becauss it maye do yowe good and can do yowe no harme for the dangere is passed as soon as yowe haue burnt the letter and i hope god will giue yowe the grace to mak good use of it to whose holy proteccion i comend yowe

To the right honorable the lord monteagle

The warning letter that revealed Catesby's plot.

The message went on to tell Lord Monteagle to burn the letter. But instead of burning it and quietly making his escape, he showed the letter to others.

A search of the cellars below the House of Lords was ordered. And in the cellars they found a man standing guard over a huge pile of

The wall is cut away to show James I and his Lords; Guy Fawkes – helped by the devil – hides in the cellar below, ready to light the gunpowder.

20

The execution of the Gunpowder Plotters.

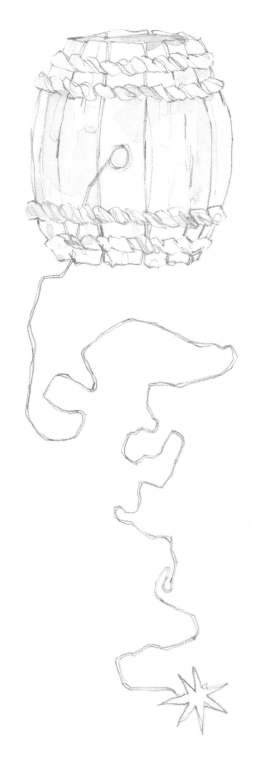

wood and coal. Underneath it were thirty-six barrels of gunpowder, connected to a slow fuse. The man, who said that his name was John Johnson, was taken before the king for questioning.

Sir Edward Hoby, a gentleman at the king's court, wrote to a friend on 19 November, to tell him what had happened:

'In a vault under the parliament chamber before spoken of, one Johnson was found . . . who, being after brought into the galleries of the court, and there demanded if he were not sorry for his so foul and heinous a treason, answered that he was sorry for nothing but that the act was not performed.'

Johnson's real name turned out to be Guy (or Guido) Fawkes, and he was one of Catesby's men. He was only involved in the plot because he was skilled in using gunpowder. Under torture, Guy Fawkes confessed his part in the plot – together with the names of Catesby and all the others involved. When they realized that the game was up, Catesby and the rest tried to get away. They were tracked down, and, in the fight which followed, four of them, including Catesby, were killed. The rest were brought back to London and stood trial with Guy Fawkes.

All of them were condemned to death.

21

OTHERS TO STUDY

James I
Robert Catesby

Oliver Cromwell

1599 – 1658

'I ... perceived a gentleman speaking (whom I knew not) very ordinarily apparelled, for it was a plain-cloth suit, which seemed to have been made by an ill country tailor: his linen was plain and not very clean ...'

Anyone might think these words were written about somebody quite ordinary. But the subject was Oliver Cromwell, a remarkable and **controversial** man, who rose from being first a **squire**, then a soldier, to be ruler of Britain.

Oliver Cromwell, the country squire who became ruler of Britain. This painting is by Samuel Cooper.

Cromwell became a **Member of Parliament** in the middle of a great quarrel between King Charles I and his Parliament. Charles believed that a king should be able to rule exactly as he pleased, and introduced unfair laws. When his Parliament disagreed with him, he ruled the country without a Parliament for eleven years.

When Parliament did meet again, the quarrel with the king went on. Charles decided to fight his enemies, and civil war broke out in Britain.

THE
Exercise of the English, in the
Militia of the Kingdome of
ENGLAND.

The title page of a leaflet about the army. You can clearly see the differences between the Roundheads (right) and the Cavaliers (left).

The king's soldiers, the Royalists (or Cavaliers), were used to fighting battles. Most of the supporters of Parliament, the Roundheads, had never fought before, and at first it seemed that King Charles would win the war. Then Oliver Cromwell, one of the leading Roundheads, helped to form the New Model Army. He trained men to be fierce soldiers – and they began to beat the king's men. The Royalist forces were crushed at the Battle of Naseby in 1645, and Cromwell became famous.

'Omens of troubled times.' It seemed to many during the Civil War that life had been turned topsy-turvy.

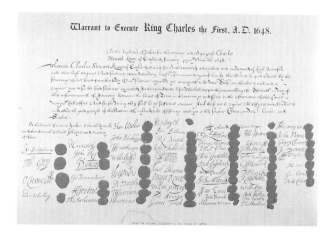

Warrant for the execution of Charles I. Oliver Cromwell's firm signature is third from the top on the left.

Many in the watching crowd wept as King Charles was executed for high treason.

DATE CHART

1599
Oliver Cromwell is born.

1628
Enters Parliament.

1642
Parliament goes to war with King Charles I.

1645
Cromwell helps to form the New Model Army after victory at Battle of Marston Moor.

1649
30 January: King Charles I is executed.

1649
Cromwell is asked to take command in Ireland.

1650
Becomes Commander-in-Chief.

1653
Made Lord Protector.

1657
Refuses the title of King.

1658
3 September: Cromwell dies.

King Charles I was captured, tried for treason, and beheaded. Oliver Cromwell, now in a position of power, played a leading part in the king's trial.

Britain now faced many problems. There was no king to rule the country. The heir to the throne, also called Charles, had fled with some of the royal family to France. Members of Parliament could not agree on how to run the country.

Cromwell realized that something must be done to get Britain back on its feet. He dismissed the Members of Parliament and took over responsibility for ruling the country.

He became Lord Protector of Britain, and was a strong and determined leader. He imposed strict **Puritan** rules. Sundays had to be spent in prayer and Bible reading; nobody could work or play games. The celebration of Christmas was banned, Catholic books and ornaments were burnt, and all the inns and theatres were closed down.

When the people of Ireland rebelled against his rule he was cruel and ruthless in his treatment of the rebels. To this day, Cromwell's name is hated in Ireland.

Cromwell's nature was full of opposites. He made many bitter enemies – 'yet did he exceed in tenderness towards sufferers', according to his servant, John Maidston.

After his death a book was written about the Civil War. It said of Cromwell:

*'In a word, as he had all the wickednesses against which damnation is denounced...
so he had some virtues...
and he will be looked upon by posterity (future generations) as a brave, bad man.'*

Cromwell ruled Britain until his death. A lot of people wanted an end to harsh Puritan rule, and were glad when King Charles I's eldest son was invited to return to Britain to be the new king, Charles II.

The new king, Charles II, rides through London to open Parliament.

OTHERS TO STUDY

**Prince Rupert
– a Royalist general.
Thomas Fairfax
– the commander of Cromwell's army.**

25

William Harvey

1578-1657

'It is clear that many of the ideas handed down by our forefathers concerning the movements and functions of the heart and of the arteries, appear ... to be full of contradictions, obscurities, or impossibilities ...'

Doctor William Harvey, who wrote these words, was a successful and highly skilled man. He had studied medicine in Italy. He was the personal doctor to both James I and Charles I. But Harvey was also a scientist with an enquiring mind.

Harvey's illustration of how the blood circulates.

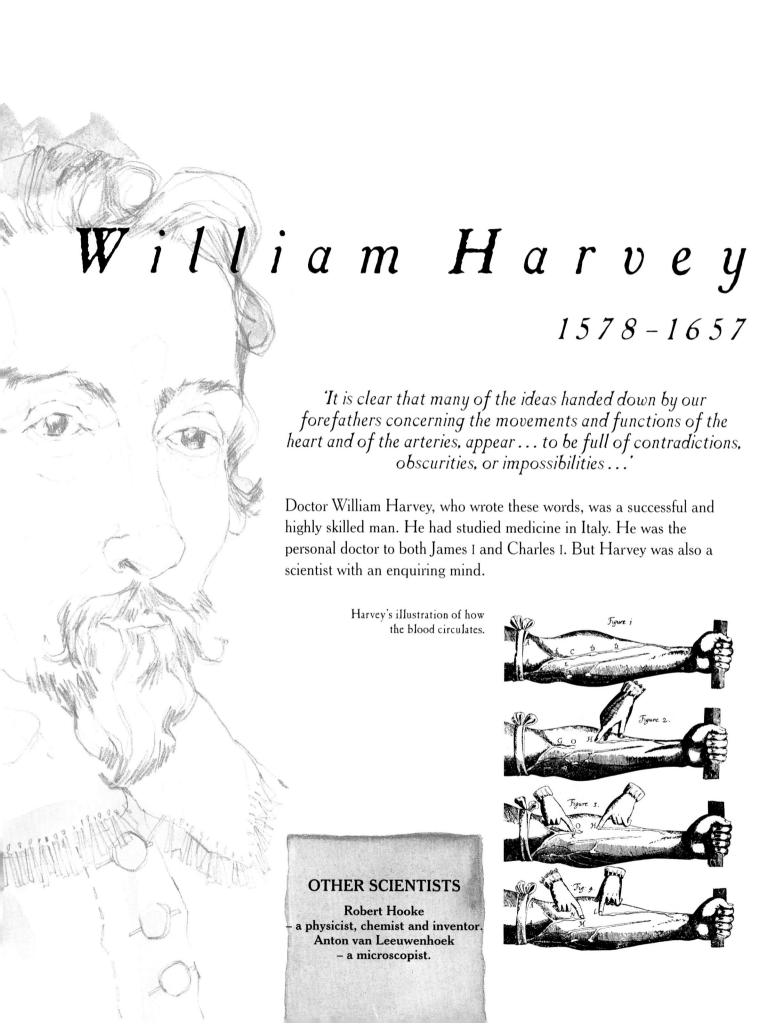

OTHER SCIENTISTS

Robert Hooke
– a physicist, chemist and inventor.
Anton van Leeuwenhoek
– a microscopist.

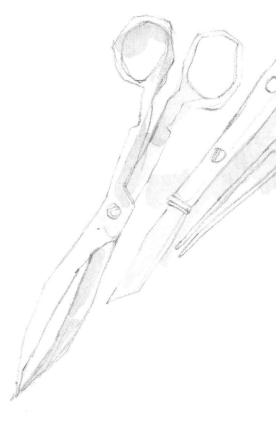

In William Harvey's day the heart, blood and **circulation** were not understood. Doctors and scientists had seen tiny flaps inside the **veins**, but did not know what they were for. They thought that blood passed directly from the right to the left side of the heart. And it was even believed that blood came partly from the liver.

Working in his own laboratory, Harvey made experiments. He discovered that the heart was a muscle, and he worked out that it must be pumping more than 200 litres of blood in an hour. And where did all that blood go to? Harvey reasoned that it must be circulating – going round and round – the body.

He realized that the little flaps he had seen in the veins were one-way valves which stopped the blood flowing backwards. He reasoned that by means of these valves, the blood must flow from the heart, through the **arteries**, to return by way of the veins.

Harvey wrote a book about his new understanding of circulation. His ideas were laughed at, however. His friend, John Aubrey, wrote:

'I have heard him say, that after his Booke of the Circulation of the Blood came out ... that 'twas beleeved by the vulgar that he was crack-brained; and all the Physitians (doctors) were against his Opinion, and envyed him; many wrote against him.'

Harvey, however, whose discoveries played a vital part in the development of medicine, lived to see his 'crack-brained' idea accepted. Aubrey went on to say:

'With much ado at last, in about twenty or thirty yeares time, it was received in all the Universities in the world; and Mr Hobbes says in his book De Corpore, he is the only man, perhaps, that ever lived to see his owne Doctrine established in his lifetime ...'

The title page from Harvey's book *De Generatione Animalium.*

DATE CHART

1578
1 April: Harvey is born at Folkestone.

1593
Admitted to Cambridge University.

1600
Goes to Padua University, Italy, as a student.

1602
Awarded a Doctor's degree at Padua; moves to London.

1604
Marries Elizabeth Browne, a doctor's daughter.

1609
Appointed as a physician at St Bartholomew's Hospital, London.

1616
Appointed as a royal physician.

1628
Publishes his theory on circulation.

1657
3 June: Harvey dies.

S a m u e l   P e p y s

1 6 3 3 – 1 7 0 3

'This day, much against my will, I did in Drury Lane see two or three houses marked with a red cross upon the doors, and "Lord have mercy upon us" writ there …'

As he sat writing his diary on 7 June, 1665, Samuel Pepys had no way of knowing that he was describing what was to be the worst outbreak of **bubonic plague** to hit Britain since the **Black Death** of 1348. Victims were shut up inside their houses, where whole families caught the sickness one after the other, and died.

People tried to stop infection by smelling herbs, swallowing potions, putting dead toads in their shirts, writing out prayers which they then swallowed – and even eating fried mice!

The opening page of Pepys's diary, which he wrote in shorthand and a mixture of languages.

28

We know now that bubonic plague is spread from the bite of fleas carried by black rats. But nobody knew this at the time, and there was no cure. The plague killed about 100,000 people throughout Britain.

Samuel Pepys, though he was very much afraid, did not catch it. He sent his wife away to the country while he carried on living in London, near his work at the Navy Office. Using shorthand, he wrote his diary nearly every day. It is largely because of him that we know so much about everyday life in the days of Charles II.

This bill of mortality tells the story of the mass burial of the thousands of plague victims in pictures as well as words.

Pepys, who came to be Secretary to the Admiralty and worked very hard at organizing the Royal Navy, enjoyed his important position. He lived life to the full – and wrote it all down.

He wrote about the money he was saving, the books and pictures he bought, the clothes he wore, the food he enjoyed and the plays he saw at the theatre. He wrote about unimportant things such as trimming the corns on his toes, hitting his thumb with a hammer while driving a nail into the wall – and what happened when the maid forgot to leave a chamber pot in his bedroom.

But Samuel Pepys's diary also tells us about the important things that happened during the nine years he kept it. After twelve years of military rule, mostly under Cromwell, Pepys sailed to Holland in the ship that brought Charles II back to Britain as its king. He went to see the new king's coronation in Westminster Abbey.

29

Londoners run to save themselves and their goods from the flames during the Great Fire in 1666.

He also described vividly the Great Fire of 1666 that started in a baker's oven and raged through London for four days and nights. Showered with flakes of hot ash, he watched the flames spread:

'. . . as far as we could see up the hill of the City, in a most horrid malicious bloody flame, not like the fine flame of an ordinary fire. We stayed till, it being darkish, we saw the fire as only one entire arch of fire from this to the other side the bridge, and in a bow up the hill, for an arch of above a mile long. It made me weep to see it.'

Victims of the plague were tipped into great pits.

30

Pepys realized that the fire could only be stopped by making a fire-break. Houses should be pulled down or blown up with dynamite before the flames reached them. He went directly to King Charles, who gave him the vital orders for the Lord Mayor. The Tower of London was only saved because the surrounding buildings were blown up.

Pepys was fortunate. The fire that burnt down 13,200 houses and eighty-nine churches, including the first St Paul's Cathedral, did not reach his house.

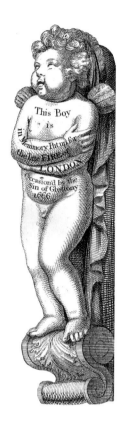

The fire that began in Pudding Lane ended at Pye Corner, Smithfield. This figure was put up there 'as a memorial of that dreadful calamity'.

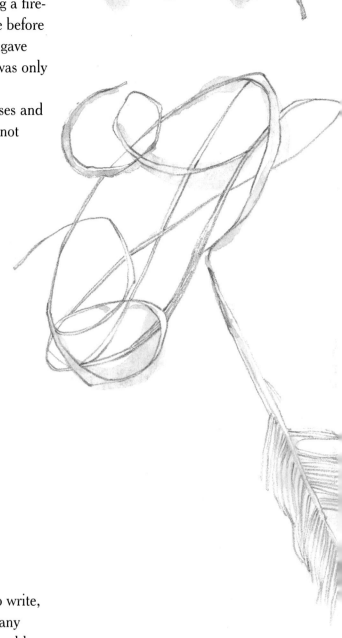

For some time Pepys had found that as soon as he started to write, especially by candlelight, his eyes ached and watered. He tried many cures, but over the next few years his eyesight grew worse. In the end he was forced to stop writing his diary, afraid that he would soon be blind. His last entry, on 31 May, 1669, ends:

'And so I betake myself to that course which is almost as much as to see myself go into my grave – for which, and all the discomforts that will accompany my being blind, the good God prepare me.'

Pepys did not go blind, though he never again kept the same kind of diary. He is remembered as the man whose writings made some of the most important years in British history come alive.

OTHER DIARISTS

John Evelyn
– an English author.
Daniel Defoe
– a novelist.

Sir Christopher Wren

1632 – 1723

'Reader, if you seek my memorial, look around you.'

These simple words are written – in Latin – on the black marble tomb of Sir Christopher Wren, in St Paul's Cathedral, London. And the magnificent building he designed is the only memorial Wren needs.

The great architect designed many superb buildings, including the Royal Observatory at Greenwich, The Sheldonian Theatre at Oxford and the Library at Trinity College, Cambridge.

But it is with the beautiful cathedral of St Paul's that Christopher Wren's name is always linked. Its splendid dome still towers above the present-day London skyline.

Wren started his career as an **astronomer**; he had even been a Professor of Astronomy at Oxford University. But, in his thirties, he discovered that designing beautiful buildings was what he really wanted to do.

Wren's Royal Hospital, Greenwich.

32

The Great Fire completely destroyed
the old St Paul's Cathedral.

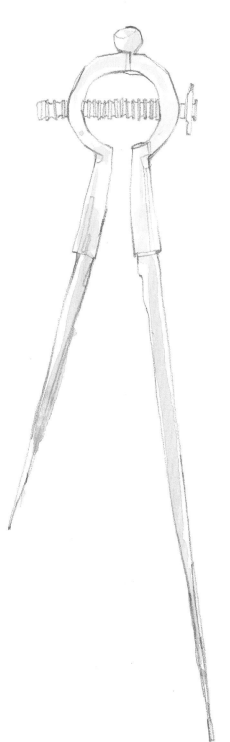

The old St Paul's had suffered a lot of damage during the Civil
War. Christopher Wren was one of a team of experts sent to the church to
decide what repairs were needed.

Wren sat down to plan a beautiful dome he wanted to add to the
old cathedral. It was the kind of work that he loved to do. He wrote:

*'I have with a great deal of pains finished the designs for it, if
they may be useful, if it happen they be not thought so I shall
not repent the great satisfaction and pleasure I have taken in
the contrivance, which equals that of poetry or compositions in
music. It hath been my constant recreation...'*

But just six days after Wren's visit to St Paul's, disaster struck. The
Great Fire of London roared through the city, destroying everything in its
path – including the ancient cathedral. His friend, John Evelyn, wrote in
his diary:

*'The stones of Paul's flew like granados (bullets), the lead
melting down the streets in a stream, and the very pavements of
them glowing with fiery redness...'*

Now, it was not just repairs that were needed. The whole building
lay in ashes.

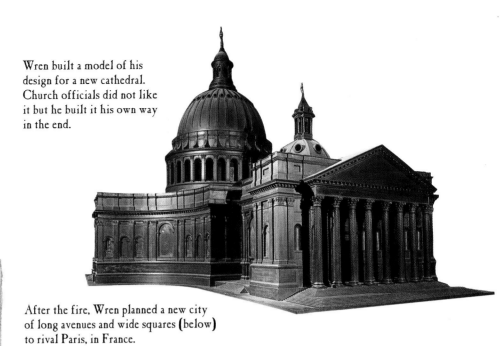

Wren built a model of his design for a new cathedral. Church officials did not like it but he built it his own way in the end.

After the fire, Wren planned a new city of long avenues and wide squares (below) to rival Paris, in France.

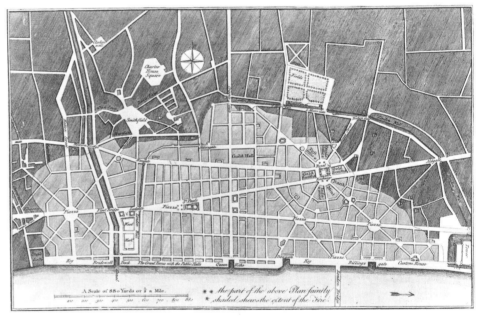

Here was a chance in a lifetime for Wren! A chance, not simply to repair the old church, but to build a completely new one. Before the ashes were cold, he began work on new plans.

His plans included not only a beautiful new cathedral, but a totally new city of wide streets, stately buildings and splendid churches. Unfortunately for Wren, there was little money to spare for such grand plans and his ideas for a new London were turned down. He did, however, design more than fifty new churches and many elegant buildings in the city.

Meanwhile, the ruins of St Paul's were unsafe and needed to be pulled down and replaced. An expert was needed, and it was agreed that Christopher Wren was the right man to take charge. The Dean of St Paul's wrote to him:

34

'Our work at the west end of St Paul's is fallen about our ears ... What we are to do next is the present deliberation, in which you are so absolutely and indispensably necessary to us, that we can do nothing, resolve on nothing without you.'

Christopher Wren took on the work. Very slowly, the ruins were cleared and building started. But it was another thirty-six years before the new St Paul's was finished.

Wren must have wondered, as the long years went by, whether he would live to see his great masterpiece. But at last, when he was seventy-eight years old, his son Christopher laid the last stone. The beautiful cathedral, Sir Christopher Wren's life's work, was completed.

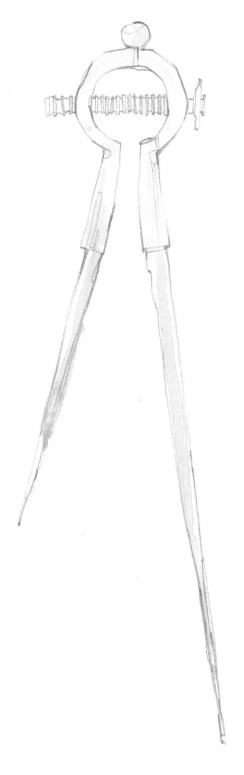

The magnificent new St Paul's – the only memorial Wren needs – rose from the ashes of London.
The dome of St Paul's Cathedral still dominates the London skyline, as you can see in the picture below.

OTHER ARCHITECTS

Inigo Jones
John Evelyn
Robert Hooke
Nicholas Hawksmoor

Sir Isaac Newton

1642 – 1727

'He very rarely went to bed till two or three of the clock, sometimes not until five or six . . . till he had finished his chemical experiments, in the performance of which he was the most accurate, strict, exact. What his aim might be I was not able to penetrate into, but his pains, his diligence at these set times made me think he aimed at something beyond the reach of human art and industry.'

Isaac Newton's secretary was right in saying that the great scientist was always aiming at something beyond his reach. His mind was always full of deep thoughts about the world, the universe, and the things around him.

Newton was perhaps the finest scientist that Britain ever produced, yet he made his greatest discoveries when he was only twenty-three. He said of himself:

Newton's coloured rings. He was fascinated by the properties of light.

36

'In those days I was in the prime of my age for invention, and minded mathematics and philosophy (studying the laws and causes of all things) more than at any time since.'

One of his discoveries came about as Newton sat in his garden one day. An apple fell from a tree, and he found himself wondering what made things fall downwards towards the earth. He reasoned that the earth must have a force which pulled things down – and his theory about the laws of **gravity** came into being.

Gravity sometimes works when we least expect it!

SIR ISAAC NEWTON LIVED HERE

Newton made a telescope that used small mirrors to reflect images of stars and planets.

Newton became interested in light. Exactly what *was* light? How did it behave? He experimented with the range, or spectrum, of the colours in light. His studies led him to build the first reflecting telescope, which was the ancestor of today's gigantic modern telescopes.

Newton's almost superhuman mind bubbled with ideas. His book on higher mathematics was so clever that few scientists of his day understood it. Many of those who did, disagreed with him. Yet mathematicians have used the **calculus** he invented ever since.

In his lifetime, Sir Isaac Newton became highly respected by everyone who knew him. He was a quiet, modest, kind man who never looked down on those who were not as clever as he was.

Towards the end of his life, Newton told his nephew:

'I do not know what I may appear to the world; but to myself I seem to have been only like a boy playing on the seashore, and diverting myself in now and then finding a smoother pebble or a prettier shell than ordinary, whilst the great ocean of truth lay all undiscovered before me.'

DATE CHART

1642
25 December: Newton is born.

1661-65
Goes to Cambridge University.

1665-66
Discovers his theory of gravity and mathematical calculus.

1671
Presents a reflecting telescope to the Royal Society.

1687
Publishes his book on mathematics, *Principia Mathematica*.

1700
Becomes Master of the Royal Mint.

1703
Becomes President of the Royal Society.

1705
Newton is knighted.

1727
Dies and is buried in Westminster Abbey.

OTHER ASTRONOMERS

Galileo Galilei
Robert Hooke
Robert Boyle
Edmond Halley

Celia Fiennes

1662 – 1741

'From hence (Uppingham) to Leicester full of sloughs, clay deep way, that I was near eleven hours going but twenty-five mile (forty-two kilometres) – as they reckon it – between Wansford and Leicester town, a footman could have gone much faster than I could ride.'

Nobody, you might think, would travel on roads as muddy as this unless they really had to. They certainly wouldn't do it for fun! But to the young Celia Fiennes a badly made, muddy road was nothing to get too upset about. She was used to such small set-backs.

In the seventeenth century, girls and women were expected to stay at home. They looked after their husbands and their homes, and raised families. They travelled rarely, except to call on their neighbours or relatives. But Celia Fiennes was not like other young women.

Celia visited the ancient monument Stonehenge. It is still standing today.

It all started when her mother suggested a holiday, for the sake of Celia's health. They left their home in Wiltshire to stay for a time with relatives in Dorset. Celia so much enjoyed visiting new places that she wanted to see even more. This was the first of many journeys she was to make.

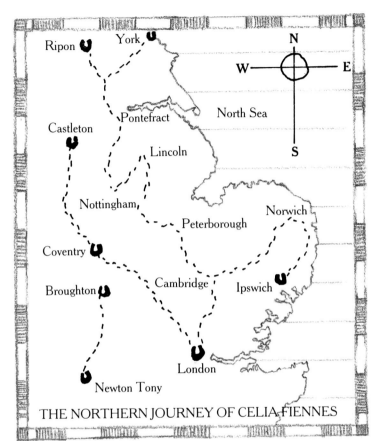

THE NORTHERN JOURNEY OF CELIA FIENNES

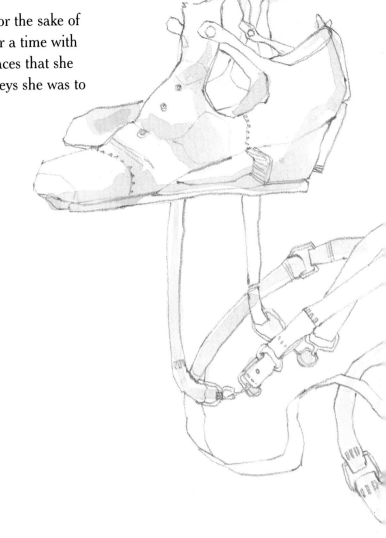

Travelling in those days was a great adventure. There were hardly any signposts and no maps. Even asking the way was sometimes hopeless:

'Generally the people here are able to give so bad a direction that passengers are at a loss what aime to take, they know scarce three mile (four and a half kilometres) *from their home...'*

During the first few years of her travels, Celia Fiennes made what she called 'small' journeys of perhaps four or five hundred kilometres. Wherever she went, she noted in her diary all the exciting things she had seen and done.

But Celia still longed to go further afield. At last, riding side-saddle on her horse and taking a couple of servants with her, she set off on her 'Great Journey'.

OTHERS TO STUDY

Daniel Defoe
– an author and journalist.
Samuel Pepys
– a diarist.
John Evelyn
– an author and diarist.

She was interested in everything. She visited a factory and watched bricks being made. She saw glass being spun into the shape of a swan – and had a go at glass spinning herself. She went to marvel at the ancient monument Stonehenge. In York she visited a mint where coins were made, and stamped a half-crown herself. In Harrogate she drank the smelly spa waters for her health:

'... the smell being so very strong and offensive that I could not force my horse near the Well...'

Celia Fiennes liked clean, modern towns. She had no time for ancient buildings. York, a town thought of today as having some very fine old streets and houses, she said had 'but a meane appearance, the Streets narrow, the houses very low'. She was happier when she got to Norwich:

'... which is walled round full of towers, except on the river side which serves for the wall; they seeme the best in repaire of any walled city I know... The whole City lookes like what it is, a rich thriveing industrious place.'

Not all Celia's experiences were pleasant. Sometimes the local food upset her stomach. Rain could turn a dry lane into a sea of sticky mud. Once she was thrown from her horse. And she had a narrow escape from **highwaymen**. Sometimes the inns she stayed at were uncomfortable. Some were so crowded that clients had to sleep three in a bed.

She was appalled by the living conditions of the poor in Scotland and on the Welsh border, where the houses were 'so decay'd that in many places ready to tumble down ...'

'Your money or your life!' Travellers were always in danger of being robbed by highwaymen like 'Mulled Sack'.

Rather prim and proper, Celia was shocked, when she visited stately homes, to see many paintings and statues of naked people. And in Bath she was glad that the ladies' bathing costumes hid their figures:

*'Your shape is not seen,
it does not cling close.'*

Celia Fiennes enjoyed her visit to the baths at Bath.

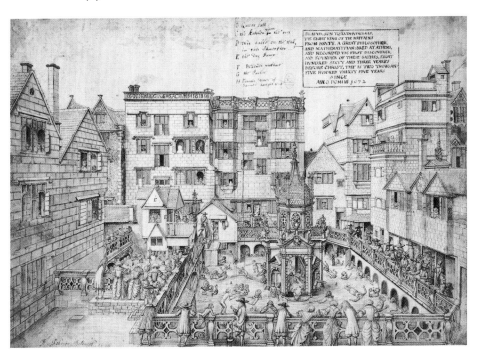

Not all Celia saw pleased her, but she was cheerful and fearless, and everything was interesting. In Somerset she wrote eagerly about the wonders of Wookey Hole Cavern, where there were **stalactites** shaped like dogs, babies and a witch.

In Cornwall she ate clotted cream and visited tin mines, where she watched men and boys hauling up the **ore** in buckets. She took away with her a piece of tin as a souvenir.

When her 'Great Journey' was ended, Celia settled down and went to live near London.

The 'Great Journey' was an exploration that took Celia Fiennes more than 2,500 kilometres. No other man or woman of her time travelled as far around Britain. Her descriptions of the towns and villages she passed through, and the people she met, give us a lively glimpse of Britain's past.

41

DATE CHART

1662
Celia Fiennes is born.

1697
May: Northern Journey.
Autumn: Tour of Kent.

1698
'Great Journey' to Newcastle
and Cornwall.

1702
Writes her impressions of
London.

1685-1703
Writes her journals.

1741
Celia dies.

Flora Macdonald

1722 - 1790

'My dear Marion, I have sent your daughter from this country, lest she should be in any way frightened with the troops lying here. She has got one Betty Burke, an Irish girl, who, as she tells me, is a good spinster. If her spinning pleases you, you can keep her till she spin all your lint...'

The night was calm and quiet. Flora Macdonald clutched this note from her stepfather to her mother. Her maid, Betty Burke, and a manservant glanced nervously around as they made their way across the shore towards the waiting boat.

Anyone watching, however, would have seen that Betty Burke was striding out almost like a man. Betty was no ordinary servant – in fact, not a woman at all, but the young prince, Charles Edward – 'Bonnie Prince Charlie' – in disguise. He was fleeing from Britain for his life.

Charles Edward's father, James Stuart, was the son of King James II, but because he was a Catholic he was not allowed to be king. James Stuart had fought for the throne, but Britain wanted no more Catholic monarchs, and his bid failed.

When Queen Anne, the last of the Stuart monarchs, died, George, a distantly related German prince, was given the throne because he was a Protestant. He became King George I. Now, his son George II was king. But Prince Charles Edward believed that the Stuarts had a better claim to the throne. He decided to fight for it. He landed in Scotland, where many loyal Highlanders joined his army. They marched down into England and fought King George's army but in the end were defeated badly. Many Scots were killed and Charles Edward himself only just escaped. Now he was on the run.

42

Hopelessly outnumbered, 'Bonnie Prince Charlie's' supporters were almost wiped out in the bloody battle of Culloden.

Flora Macdonald, a young woman who had been brought up in the Isle of Skye, was very loyal to Charles Edward. She once told Colonel O'Neil, a friend who had fought in the prince's army, that she had never met the prince, but 'a sight of him would make her happy, tho' he was on a hill and she on another'.

Colonel O'Neil asked Flora to help Charles Edward to escape to France. She knew that if they were caught she would be killed, but she agreed.

They decided that the prince should dress as a woman and pretend to be Flora's maid. Flora helped Charles Edward into a lilac-flowered dress, apron and cloak. MacEachain, a trusted family member, wrote:

'The company being gone, the Prince . . . was dressed by Miss Flora in his new attire, but he could not keep his hands from adjusting his head-dress, which he cursed a thousand times.'

In great danger all the way, the boat was rowed towards Skye. The next morning they were seen by soldiers, but the boatmen rowed away as fast as they could out of musket range and the boat landed safely on the island.

Flora was later caught and questioned, and sent to London as a prisoner. Nothing was ever proved against her, however, and when the rebellion was finally over she was set free. She never saw the prince again. Flora became a heroine in Scotland because of her great courage.

Prince Charles Edward finally managed to escape to France. He never became king, and spent the rest of his life in Europe. He began to drink heavily, and in the end died an alcoholic.

The boat that carried 'Bonnie Prince Charlie' away to the Isle of Skye signalled the end of the last attempt by the Stuarts to regain the British throne.

DATE CHART

1722
Flora Macdonald is born.

1745
Charles Edward lands in Scotland.

1745
October: Charles's army begins to march south.

1746
April: the English defeat the Scottish at Culloden.
29 June: Flora and Charles land near Kilbride Point, Skye. Flora is put in custody.
19 September: Charles escapes on a boat for France.

1748
Flora is released.

1751
Marries Allan Macdonald.

1788
Prince Charles Edward dies.

1790
Flora dies.

OTHERS TO STUDY

Prince James Stuart
– a claimant to the British throne.
Prince William Augustus
– a brutal English general.

G l o s s a r y

Adultery Breaking the Christian marriage promise to be faithful to your wife or husband.

Arteries Narrow tubes which carry blood from the heart to all the parts of the body.

Astronomer A scientist who studies the movements of stars and planets.

Black Death A form of bubonic plague which killed thousands of people in 1348.

Bubonic Plague An infectious disease spread by rat fleas.

Calculus A mathematical system of calculation.

Catholics Christians who belong to the Roman Catholic Church. They believe that their leader, the Pope, is God's messenger on the earth.

Cavalry Soldiers who fight on horseback.

Circulation The movement of blood around the body.

Colonists A group of people who settle in a different country to their own.

Controversial A word used to describe someone or something whose actions are likely to cause arguments.

Coronation The crowning ceremony of a king or queen.

Divorce The ending of a marriage by law.

Gravity The force that pulls objects towards the earth.

Highwaymen People, usually on horseback, who stopped and robbed travellers on the road.

House of Lords A group of nobles in the English Parliament, who pass or reject new laws.

Mary Tudor A Catholic queen of England from 1553 to 1558. She was known as 'Bloody Mary' because she had many Protestants executed.

Member of Parliament Someone who is elected to represent people in Parliament.

Miscarriage When a baby is born too early and does not survive.

Ore Rock or mineral from which metals can be obtained.

Parliament Two groups of politicians, the House of Commons and the House of Lords, who make the British laws.

Protestants Christians who do not belong to the Catholic Church.

Puritans Very strict Protestants who disapproved of entertainment, such as music and dancing, and decorations in churches.

Royal Society An association founded by Charles II in 1660, to encourage scientific research.

Scaffold A raised wooden platform on which executions were carried out.

Spanish Armada A great fleet of ships sent by King Philip II of Spain to invade England in 1588. The Armada was defeated by English ships.

Squire Someone who owned an estate, with a manor house, farms and land.

Stalactites Icicle-shaped formations that hang from the roofs of caves. They are made of solidified drips of water containing lime.

Treason A crime against the ruler or government of a country.

Veins Very thin, long tubes that carry the blood round inside the body and back to the heart.

Books to read

M. Carter, C. Culpin and N. Kinloch,
  Past into Present 2: 1400-1700
  (Collins Educational, 1990)
Journey Through History series
  (Wayland, 1993-94)
H. Middleton, *Every Day Life in the Sixteenth Century*
  (Macdonald, 1992)

T. D. Triggs, *Tudor and Stuart Times* (Folens, 1992)
T. D. Triggs, *Tudor Britain* (Wayland, 1992)
Tudors and Stuarts series (Wayland, 1993-94)
T. Wood, *The Stuarts* (Ladybird, 1991)
R. Wright, *Craft Topics: Tudors* and *Stuarts* (Watts, 1993)

Places to visit

Anne Boleyn
Hampton Court Palace, Richmond, London. Tel: (081) 781 9500
Tower of London. Tel: (071) 709 0765

Lady Jane Grey
Bradgate House, Bradgate Park, Leicester. Tel: (0533) 362713
  Home of Lady Jane Grey.

Sir Walter Raleigh
British Museum, London. Tel: (071) 636 1555
  Houses Raleigh's *History of the World*.
National Maritime Museum, Greenwich, London.
  Tel: (081) 858 4422

William Shakespeare
Shakespeare Globe Museum, London. Tel: (071) 928 6342
Shakespeare's birthplace and Anne Hathaway's cottage,
  Stratford-upon-Avon. Tel: (0789) 204016

Guy Fawkes
Ashmolean Museum, Oxford. Tel: (0865) 278000
  Houses Guy Fawkes' lantern.

Oliver Cromwell
Cromwell Museum, Huntingdon. Tel: (0480) 425830
Newbury district Museum, Newbury, Berkshire.
  Tel: (0635) 30511
  Audio-visual display of Civil War battles.

William Harvey
The Harvey Chapel, Hempstead parish church, Essex.
Whipple Museum of the History of Science, Cambridge.
  Tel: (0223) 334540

Samuel Pepys
Eyam Hall, Eyam, Derbyshire. Tel: (0433) 631976
  A village that sealed itself off during the plague.
Museum of London, London Wall, London. Tel: (071) 600 3699
  The Great Fire Experience.

Sir Christopher Wren
St Paul's Cathedral, London. Tel: (071) 248 2705
Trinity College, Cambridge. Tel : (0223) 338400

Sir Isaac Newton
Old Royal Observatory, Greenwich, London. Tel: (081) 858 4422
Whipple Museum of the History of Science, Cambridge.
  Tel: (0223) 334540

Celia Fiennes
The Building of Bath Museum, Bath. Tel: (0225) 333895
Poldark Mine and Heritage Complex, near Helston, Cornwall.
  Tel: (0326) 573173

Flora Macdonald
Culloden. Tel: (0542) 40757
  Site of the 1746 defeat of Charles Edward Stuart.
West Highland Museum, Fort William. Tel: (0397) 702169
  Relics of Charles Edward Stuart.

I n d e x